The Facemakers

Linda Blake

W0462742

Mursia
MODULO
Cornelsen
WEILIN+GÖÖS
ASCHEHOUG
KALEIDOSCOPE

THE FACEMAKERS (Fiction Factory 30)

This book is a part of the series FICTION FACTORY. See list of already published titles page 56.

A sound cassette is available for each title.

Danish ISBN:	978-87-7565-519-9	Norwegian ISBN:	82-03-XXXXX-X
Swedish ISBN:	91-542-06985-0	Italian ISBN:	88-425-8396-0
German ISBN:	978-3-464-06985-1	Canadian ISBN:	2-89113-XXX-X
Finnish ISBN:	951-35-XXXX-X		

Heat, Sand and Rocks

There was desert all around her for as far as she could see. Nothing but sand, dust, rocks and bare hills. Occasionally there would be an ugly, twisted, dead tree and a few dry bushes here and there. Tracey hated the place, and if the devil had appeared and offered her a bath in return for her soul she would have said 'yes' without a second thought.

Coming into the 'outback' with Charlie Moore had been a big mistake. In fact she wished she'd never come to Australia at all. The intense light was hurting her million dollar eyes like hell. She had forgotten her sunglasses back at the miserable hotel. Her silky, smooth skin was getting dangerously dry. Her long, black hair looked terrible and in the morning she had found things; insects, with wings, crawling around in it. The sand was as fine as flour, and the worst thing about the whole trip. The sand got absolutely everywhere. It was in her ears, her mouth, her nose and she could taste it on her tongue. After three days in the 'outback', Tracey felt like every hole in her body was full of dust.

Tracey picked up the big, plastic can of water. She hoped Charlie couldn't see her. She poured the water over her head and let it run down her face and down her body. It felt absolutely wonderful, and, for a few seconds, she forgot where she was and drifted away. Away to a beautiful, cool Arabian oasis somewhere on the caravan route to Mecca. But then Tracey opened her eyes once more and saw where she really was. Her head started to throb and buzz again because of the heat. She had taken some painkillers and washed them down with beer, but her head still hurt. It was easily thirty-five degrees and getting hotter all the time.

Charlie had only given Tracey five minutes to change her clothes, comb her hair, and get her make-up just right. She looked at her plastic watch. It felt like it was melting in the sun. Time was running out for them. Charlie, who had talked her into coming out into the desert, was getting increasingly irritated.

"Hurry up, will you, Tracey? We're losing the light. I don't want to spend another day out here!"

The thought of spending another day in the desert made Tracey's head spin. She tore off the shirt and the rest of her clothes.

"I'm going as quick as I can, Charlie."

"Well, go quicker, Tracey!"

There were times when Tracey wanted to strangle Charlie Moore. When she had been at school, like lots of young girls, she'd dreamt about being a successful model. Now she was one, and she realised how different the reality of the job was from her youthful dreams. There was a lot more to being a top model than just looking beautiful, wearing beautiful clothes, travelling all over the world and eventually marrying a millionaire rockstar.

Today there were no dreams, only reality and damn hard work. It was an absolute nightmare. She was standing stark naked behind a jeep in the great Australian desert and she was dead tired. The last thing she wanted to do was to smile for the camera and put on a skin-tight, black plastic dress. Tracey waved the flies away from her beautiful, famous face. There seemed to be hundreds of the little devils buzzing around her. One dived into her mouth like a mad kamikaze pilot and she spat it out. Then something really enormous, with red and yellow stripes and great, flapping wings, landed on her naked stomach. Tracey had never seen anything like it before, anywhere in the world. And then the monster stuck something into her that felt like a red hot sword! Tracey screamed, grabbed it and crushed it angrily between her hands. Blood spurted out of its fat body like water from a tiny fountain. For a moment she thought she was going to be sick.

Charlie shouted from the other side of the jeep. He sounded even more irritated now.

"What's up now, Tracey?"

"Some huge insect just bit a lump out of me, Charlie. It was as big as a bird!"

"Oh don't go on like that, Tracey. We haven't got much time left. Hurry up for God's sake!"

Tracey vowed to herself that she would never, ever, do Charlie Moore a favour again. This was the last time. Now she had paid him back for the help he'd given her at the beginning of her modelling career back in England.

But Tracey was a professional and she wasn't going to give up. She washed her hands and squeezed her way into the horrible plastic dress. It was hot and very sticky inside it. Tracey felt like she was wearing a plastic rubbish bag. The thing was so tight it was difficult to breathe. The stupid dress was just too small and her breasts fell out of the top of the thing.

Suddenly the cheap-looking, metal zipper at the front burst open all the way down to her navel. This was the straw that broke the lady camel's back. Tracey rushed out from behind the Jeep and looked around for Charlie. Charlie had lived too long!

Charlie was sitting on the ground in the shade created by the jeep and he was putting a new film in his camera. He looked up at her and smiled in his good-natured way. Tracey knew what he was looking at and she tried to pull the front of the dress together. It was hopeless so she just pulled the stupid thing over her head, threw it down on the ground and stamped on it.

"I must say I like the view, Tracey. I always thought you had a wonderful body. 'My Venus from the King's Road,' I used to call you. The only problem is, these photographs are not for Playboy. Still I can keep them for my private collection. Is that all right with you?"

"Cut out the 'humour', Charlie. I'm sweating like a pig and smell like a camel's armpit. I want to go back to Victoria Springs and get the first plane back to Sydney."

"We haven't finished yet, Tracey, and that 'dress' you're standing on is extremely expensive, you know."

"Yeah, and it's got a useless zipper. This place is like hell on earth. I'll never forgive you for this."

"I didn't say coming out here was going to be easy, Tracey. In the old days you could change your clothes in the back of a taxi going from one job to another. Don't you remember that terrible time we had in Iceland when I drove into that enormous snow drift? You never used to complain so much. You must be getting soft, or is it because you're famous now?"

"Charlie, I don't want to get all sentimental about the past. This place is a hole and I want to go back to the hotel. I'm really tired, Charlie. Please can we pack up and get out of here?"

"All right, Tracey. Forget about the plastic dress and we'll finish off with that long, yellow silk thing. Go and stand over by that old, twisted tree when you're ready."

"Are you serious? After everything I just said!"

"Look, Tracey, we've got to finish. You're a professional. You're ambitious and tough as steel when you have to be. I've always respected you for that. You've a positive attitude and a good personality. I've always liked girls with a sense of humour. Come on, Tracey. I can't think of any more compliments. Let's finish. What do you say?"

Charlie gave Tracey one of his biggest smiles and she gave up being angry with him. When he smiled like that he looked thirty, not forty.

"All right, Charlie. Sweet words will get you everywhere with me. Just give me three minutes."

Tracey went back behind the jeep and poured more water over herself trying to cool herself. She dried herself on the same towel she'd been using for the last three days and put on the yellow silk dress. It was cool, soft and very beautiful. Tracey thought that she would like to keep it. She brushed her long, dark hair quickly ran her fingers through it and shook her head from side to side. Then she fixed her make-up, changed the colour of her lipstick and fixed-up her eyes. When she was finished she ran over to the tree where Charlie was waiting and put a pair of crystal-clear high heels on. Tracey looked at Charlie and gave him one of her best and most expensive smiles.

"You look fabulous, Tracey. Now give me some great poses and we'll be finished in ten minutes. I promise you."

Once she was in front of the camera Tracey's

attitude totally changed. Charlie was right, she was a professional. She turned this way and that way. Smiled and licked her lips, opened her mouth perfectly, bent and twisted her long, slim body just perfectly.

"Yeah, yeah, that's great, Tracey. You've still got what it takes. Beautiful, now hold that position while I change cameras. Don't move a muscle or a hair on your head!"

The Wrong Way

Charlie took more than an hour's worth of film before he was satisfied. Tracey didn't have the strength to say anything. She was just cruising now on automatic pilot. When they were finished she walked back to the jeep, slipped out of the silk dress and changed back into her own clothes. A pair of old jeans she'd bought off a real cowboy in Texas and a shirt she'd found in a little market town in the Mexican mountains. Then she climbed into the jeep and closed her eyes. Charlie packed all his equipment away and got in beside her. He started the jeep's powerful engine and soon they were heading back along the dusty desert track towards Victoria Springs.

"I really appreciate you doing this shoot for me, Tracey. I need the money, you see. I think I only got this job because I knew you and you said you'd wear the clothes."

"It's all right, Charlie. I had a few days off so I had the time."

"You don't have to lie to me, Tracey. I know exactly how busy your bureau keeps you.

You're a hot name and everyone wants to make a lot of money out of you."

"I make a lot of money too, Charlie. I can ask for five thousand pounds a day now. Nobody makes me do anything I don't want to. I have a bit of power now, so I can pick and choose what I want. I'm privileged."

"Anyway, I really, really, appreciate this, Tracey. When I called you up I was afraid you wouldn't remember me, or you'd just say 'no' you were too busy. I was afraid you'd become a real 'Prima dona', a 'supermodel'."

"No, not yet. But I'm on the way. The bureau thinks I'll be able to earn some really big money in a couple of years."

"Good for you, Tracey."

They drove on in silence for a few minutes and Tracey began to feel bad about talking so much about money and success. She had heard that Charlie had financial problems. Then he said:

"It's great to see you again, Tracey. I always liked you. Not just because you're beautiful."

"Charlie, if you need money why don't you come on back to England? I've got lots of contacts. People still remember your name, I'm sure of it. I could help you along."

"No way, Tracey!"

"Why not, Charlie?

"The truth is I get depressed as hell every time I visit England. Back in the sixties and seventies there was so much life and energy in London. I disliked the eighties, but there was still some life. Now things are terrible."

"Things aren't that bad, Charlie."

"No, you don't really understand. Back when I was starting out in the seventies, I really felt London was the centre of the universe. The whole country looked like it was going to change and get better. Young people had jobs, money, music and clothes and there was so much happening. It seemed like there were no limits to what we could do. But England's changed. All the doors we started to push open, well, they've shut tight again. I never dreamt I would see time move backwards. It's scary, Tracey."

"I've never heard you talk that before, Charlie. So you're a kind of exile, Charlie."

"I haven't thought about it like that, but you're right. For me Australia represents the future and England's the past. The last time I was in England I could feel the frustration and violence bubbling under the surface. I just don't want to be there when things explode."

"Jesus, Charlie, you sound so depressing. Like I said, things aren't that bad. All this sun has affected your head. You've become a real philosopher. Next you'll move into a cave in the mountains like a hermit!"

"I'm sorry, Tracey. Being in the desert makes me think. Think about my life and what I'm doing with it. I come out into the desert a lot now."

"Well, I hope I don't start to think. I gave up thinking when I started modelling."

"Other people think for you, do they?"

"No, they don't, Charlie. I'm just very busy."

"Busy making lots of money."

"Yeah, and what's wrong with that?"

Charlie looked at her and gave her a weak smile.

"Nothing, Tracey. Are you happy?"

"Happy? I don't have time to think about 'happiness', Charlie. I broke up with Rico de Alverada at Christmas."

"Isn't he that Spanish film maker? The one who makes films full of beautiful young girls and handsome men?"

"Rico's a very positive person, Charlie. He loves beautiful places and things and people. I don't think he'll ever make a great film. Rico hasn't got anything he really wants to say. Nothing makes Rico angry."

"So you're all alone now? Any chance for me again?"

"I don't like to see time go backwards either, Charlie."

"Sorry, Tracey, I have to try. I mean here I am, sitting next to one of the most beautiful women in the whole world."

Tracey acted like she hadn't heard him. There was no point starting the old argument up again. Right after they first met she had told him that she was never going to become his girlfriend, but she would always be his friend, if that was enough.

They drove onwards for over three quarters of an hour across the desert, and nobody said a word. Tracey pulled the map out and looked at it. Then she looked to where the sun was slowly sinking behind the hills on the horizon.

"Yea, what's the matter?"

"Stop the jeep a minute, Charlie. This can't be the right way. We should have reached the road by now. Where is that old bridge we crossed this morning?"

Charlie stopped the jeep. He took the map from Tracey and studied it carefully.

"You're right, Tracey. We're going the wrong way. I don't understand how it could have happened. We'll have to cut across over that way and get to the road. I hope the track isn't too bad. Still, the jeep's got four-wheel-drive and I've been out in the desert before."

"Can't we just radio for help, Charlie? Maybe somebody can send a helicopter for me."

"Just for you?"

"Yeah, I've got to get back to Sydney."

"Listen, we're not lost, Tracey, and we're not in trouble. This isn't a real emergency. We can't call up the authorities just because you want to get home early!"

"All right, Charlie, I understand. I just really need a bath."

"You always smell nice to me, Tracey."

"Seriously, Charlie, you promised that we'd be back in Victoria Springs tonight. I want to go back to Sydney tomorrow. The plane leaves at ten in the morning from Victoria Springs, doesn't it?"

"Ten o'clock tomorrow, that's right. Look, don't worry, Tracey. I'll get you back tonight for your bath. There should be a route through those hills over there. I think If we cut across that way we can reach the road, and we won't have to go back the way we came."

Charlie started the jeep again and they turned towards the hills.

Over and Out

At first the track was not too bad; a bit rough, but the jeep was built for this type of terrain. Tracey began to relax. It looked like they were going to reach Victoria Springs by midnight. Unfortunately, the track was getting worse. There were bumps and holes everywhere. Charlie was driving too fast as well.

"Drive a bit slower, Charlie. I'm starting to feel sick."

"Sorry, Tracey. I usually drive fast when I'm out in the desert."

"You really like it out here in the desert, don't you, Charlie?"

"You're right, Tracey. Yeah, When I'm out here I feel free."

Charlie drove more slowly for a few minutes, but then he began to increase speed once more. Tracey held on tightly and tightened her safety-belt. She hoped that they would reach the road soon, before her teeth were shaken out of her head.

It was getting dark very quickly and the

track was difficult to see. They were climbing upwards along the side of a hill. When Tracey looked out of the window she could only see for a couple of metres. The jeep was surrounded by darkness. Charlie didn't seem to care. Tracey was about to tell him to slow down again, when, suddenly, the track turned violently to the left, and she saw that it had suddenly disappeared! There was only darkness in front of them. Charlie swore at the top of his voice and shouted:

"The rain must have washed the track away! Hang on, Tracey!"

He slammed on the brakes, but it was too late. The jeep plunged into nothing but air and then it fell downwards. It crashed to the ground with a violent crunch, bounced into the air and crashed down again. Charlie and Tracey bounced around inside like rubber balls in a bucket. The jeep jerked forward again and then the nose went down. The steering wheel spun out of control in Charlie's hands. The jeep turned to the left and rushed down the hillside. Charlie was spitting out swear words and trying to regain control. The brakes had failed. He tried the hand brake and then tried putting the jeep in a lower gear. There was a terrible sound of metal teeth grinding on metal teeth.

Now, everything seemed to be happening very quickly. The jeep shuddered and slowed down slightly, but then one of the front wheels snapped off. The jeep swerved violently, tipped over onto its roof and began to roll down the hillside.

Tracey felt like they rolled for hours, but, in reality, only seconds were passing. Miraculously, it stopped rolling and fell onto its wheels again. Then it crashed headlong into a large rock at the bottom of the hillside.

All the windows exploded. Glass flew around inside the jeep like snowflakes in a blizzard. Tracey covered her face and eyes with her hands. Charlie wasn't as quick as Tracey and glass struck his face. Tracey felt her head hit the side of the jeep and suddenly darkness surrounded her. She felt as if she was sinking into a bottomless black hole. Down and down she fell into nothing.

When Tracey finally opened her eyes, she was alone. She remembered what had happened, but where the hell was Charlie? She couldn't understand why he hadn't helped her out of the jeep. Tracey tried to open the door, but it was jammed, so she climbed out through the shattered window screen and down onto the ground.

She stood looking around but she couldn't see Charlie anywhere. There was a full moon now, but the silvery light didn't help much. Tracey realised that they had been very lucky. Lucky, because the jeep hadn't caught on fire and exploded with them still inside.

"Charlie? Come on, Charlie; answer me. Where the hell are you?"

There was no answer from Charlie. Tracey tried hard not to panic. Crying and screaming wouldn't do any good, not out here. This wasn't an accident on the motorway outside London or on the freeway in L.A. Tracey stumbled back to the jeep and opened the door at the back. Everything had been thrown about and was in a terrible jumble.

It took her a few minutes, but finally she found the torch and switched it on. She saw her make-up box and opened it to look at her face. It looked like something out of a horror film, covered in streaks of blood. Tracey shivered and saw that she had a bad cut on her forehead, just below her hairline. Then she went around to the other side of the jeep and shouted. There was no answer, only the echo of her own voice coming back to her.

Tracey moved forward slowly. The ground dropped away steeply in front of her. She looked on both sides and it was the same. Then she understood. She was standing a couple of feet from the edge of a river. Only there was no water. The riverbed had completely dried-up.

Suddenly, Tracey heard a low groan directly in front of her. She began to scan over the riverbed with the torch. The beam of yellow light made her feel safer. It was a primitive feeling, but it was still a good feeling to have. She pointed the beam of torchlight towards the sound and found Charlie's body. He was lying flat on his back, about fifteen feet below her, at the bottom of the riverbed. Tracey realised that Charlie must have left the jeep after the crash, stumbled around in the darkness, and then fallen down into the riverbed.

She scrambled down the bank and ran over to him. One of his legs looked strange and twisted. Tracey wasn't an expert, but she was sure his leg was broken and the rest of him didn't look too good either. She touched his face with her shaking fingers and spoke to him.

"Charlie, Charlie, open your eyes, please, love."

He opened his eyes and looked up at her.

"Is this heaven?"

"No, it's the other place. How are you feeling?"

"Terrible, Tracey. Where are we?"

"At the bottom of a dried-up riverbed."

"I'm freezing cold, Tracey."

"Wait a minute and I'll get you something to keep you warm from the jeep."

Tracey climbed the steep bank and returned to the jeep. She looked around for a blanket, only there was no blanket. But there was a mountain of high-fashion clothes. Tracey grabbed as many as she could carry in her arms and rushed back to Charlie. She covered him with six beautiful dresses and folded one into a pillow to put under his head.

"How does that feel? Better?" she asked.

"It feels very expensive, the guy who designed those clothes will have a heart attack when he hears about this."

"It'll be the first time anyone has found real use for his clothes. That's for sure."

Charlie laughed, then he coughed and shivered. Tracey could see he was still cold.

"Do you think I can make the radio work and contact someone for help?"

"Yeah, just switch it on and press the emergency button. It's automatically programmed to send out an S.O.S. on all frequencies. It's nice to know that technology can help you when you really need it."

Tracey went back to the jeep and found the radio hidden under more clothes. Unfortunately, it looked more smashed up than Charlie did. She switched it on and pressed the emergency button, but nothing happened. She picked it up and shook it. Something was rattling around inside. Tracey went back and told Charlie the bad news.

"That certainly is going to make things more difficult, Tracey."

"Yeah, are you still cold, Charlie?"

"I'm turning into a big, lump of ice and my leg hurts like blazes. I think it's broken."

"Wait a minute, Charlie. I'll soon get you warm."

"What are you doing, Tracey?"

"Sssh, lie back and enjoy it."

"I'm not going anywhere, Tracey."

Tracey crawled under the dresses to Charlie and pressed herself up against his cold body. She took his hands and began to blow on them and rub them warm.

"This is close to heaven, Tracey. I used to dream about this happening."

"I'm glad to hear your famous sense of humour hasn't left you. Only save your strength, we'll have a lot to do tomorrow. We have to think about how we're going to get out of here."

"I don't think I will be going anywhere, Tracey. I can't feel my legs anymore. Do you think my back's broken?"

"No, your back isn't broken. It can't be. I don't think... I'm sure it isn't broken. Now try to get some sleep, Charlie."

Charlie was silent for a few minutes. Tracey held him in her arms and tried to warm him and give him some of her strength.

"I can't sleep, Tracey. I keep thinking..."

"What about, we can't do anything until morning."

"I... I think I'm going to die."

"Of course you're not going to die, Charlie. I won't let you die. How can you be so selfish thinking like that? If you die I'll be all on my own. Tomorrow when it gets light we'll think of something."

"I'm going to die, Tracey. I'm afraid. Hold me closer!"

Tracey pressed herself closer to Charlie and

stroked his face with her fingers.

"I'm scared, Tracey. The desert is so enormous... and we're so... so small. I mean, what are we really compared to nature? We're just so small... so small and insignificant."

Tracey could feel Charlie's body shivering and she was sure the pain and the shock were affecting his mind. He kept on talking for a long time and she could only understand half of what he was saying. Finally, he seemed to get tired and stopped. Then he suddenly said he was going to die and started to cry like a child.

"Charlie, listen to me. All you have to do is lie here next to me and not give up hope. We are not going to die in the desert."

"You don't know anything about the desert, Tracey. You're a beautiful girl who looks good on film. The camera likes you, Tracey. That's all. You don't know much about how hard life can be."

"Charlie, you don't really know anything about me or where I come from. I haven't always been a model. I had a life before I met you."

"Really? Tell me about it."

They lay together for a long time and slowly Charlie's body got warmer. She could feel that he wasn't asleep.

"Speak to me, Tracey, say something, please. I'm afraid."

"All right, I'll tell you a story, Charlie. It's a true story about a girl I used to know."

Concrete Streets

"When I was almost fifteen I met a boy at a disco. His name was Pete and he was eighteen. He was the first real boyfriend I ever had. He lived close to the block of flats where I lived with my parents."

"My father lost his job soon after I met Pete and losing his job really changed him. He started to get depressed and angry, and he started to drink too much. My dad spent so much time watching television, it's a miracle his eyes didn't turn square. Things started to go wrong at home between me and my parents. There were lots of fights and arguments. Anyway, my dad hated Pete. He was always criticising him and me. I don't know why. Maybe he would have hated anyone who came near me. My mum was always on my dad's side. I think she was afraid of him".

"I was tired of school too. I just didn't see the point of studying all the time. There were no jobs."

"One day I had a terrible row with my father and he threw me out of our flat and told me not to come back. I remember I sat down in the little kids playground below our block of flats, and, when I looked up, I saw my clothes floating down from my bedroom window. My dad had just thrown them out of the window. I collected up what I could carry and visited a friend of mine called Julie. She was a couple of years older than me and she had a baby called Desmond. I only stayed with her for a couple of days."

"Pete came to see me and we talked about what to do. He said he had friends who had moved down to London and they were having a great time. There were jobs in London and loads of things to do. Pete said we could stay with them and we could be together and nobody could tell us what to do anymore. So we hitched to London in a truck carrying chickens. I was really excited about going to London and starting a new life with Pete. I really believed everything was going to be great. We'd get a room in Pete's friend's house, we'd get jobs and a bit of money and be together."

"I thought we could be happy. I didn't think things could be worse in London than back home. I was wrong. I must have been really stupid. I think it was because Pete was the first person I'd ever been in love with. I really wanted to believe everything he told me. I wanted everything to be true."

"Things started to go wrong right from the beginning. We went to the house where Pete's friends lived only they didn't live there anymore. The house was a real slum too. We asked around and found out that nobody knew where they moved. So Pete and I had nowhere to sleep and no real friends in a big, big city."

"We soon found out that everything in London was amazingly expensive. The first night we didn't sleep at all, we just wandered around the streets looking at the empty shop windows. There were people sleeping in the streets. I never knew that so many people slept on the streets in London. There were men and women next to one another in shop doorways. Pete said we would never end up like them."

"We tried to find work, but it was so difficult. After a couple of days we'd used up all our money. People on the street said we should try asking tourists for money. Say we needed money for cigarettes or a cup of coffee. Pete never got very much, but people seemed to like me. Pete said it was because I was prettier than he was."

"After a week we found a place to sleep in a

little park. Every night we'd climb through a hole in the fence and we'd sleep on a wooden bench, near some bushes. The bench was under a big tree and the tree kept the rain off us. We'd put all our clothes on and cover ourselves with a couple of black plastic rubbish sacks. That bench under the tree was our first 'home'."

"During the daytime we put all our things in the rubbish bags and we'd hide them in the bushes behind our bench. Then we'd go out and start begging on the streets of Central London. On a good day I sometimes begged four or five pounds."

"One day we met a really nice man in Euston station. He said Pete reminded him of his son. We told him about ourselves and he gave us some money. He also said he might be able to help us find somewhere to live, but it would take a bit of time. That was the first piece of luck we'd had since we arrived in London, and that night we felt like there was a light at the end of the tunnel for us. We started to make all sorts of crazy plans about the future."

"Then I started to be sick in the mornings. I went to the doctor and found out I was going to have a baby. I was three months pregnant and it was a real surprise. I just couldn't believe it was happening to me. I thought I was too young to get pregnant. The doctor told me to go back home. He said sleeping out in the cold was dangerous for me and the baby. He said I had to find somewhere decent to live."

"We went down to the social security office and told them I was pregnant and that I had to have somewhere to live. The social worker told me to go back home to Manchester. She said there was a ten year waiting list for a council flat. There was nothing she could do to help me. She asked me my age and then she put me on a special emergency housing list. She also said she might be able to get me into a bed and breakfast hotel and I should come back in few days. But I was afraid she would get the police to send me home or take the baby away because I was so young, so I didn't go back anymore."

"We carried on sleeping on our bench in the park. One night we found someone else sleeping on it. He wouldn't move and Pete had a fight with him. I'd never seen Pete hit anyone. I didn't know he could be so violent. He lost all self-control and started to punch and kick this

old tramp like crazy. I thought he was going to kill him. I dragged Pete off him and the old tramp just crawled away. I was crying and almost hysterical. It was so stupid. It was only an old bench under a tree. They were fighting about a park bench under a tree!"

"Then one day we came back and found that all our things had been stolen from under the bushes. Everything we had was gone. All our clothes, soap, toothbrushes, biscuits, a few cans of Coke. We felt so miserable. How can people steal from the poor? Pete got really depressed and said he felt like jumping in the River Thames with a rock around his neck. I managed to talk him out of it and told him to think about the baby. He just said there was no point having a baby in such a rotten world, but I told him I was going to have the baby, and be a good mother to it."

"The same day, in Oxford Street, we had some luck. Our first piece of luck for a long time. Outside the underground station we bumped into the old gentleman we'd met before at Euston Station. He looked pleased to see us and was friendly and sympathetic. He bought us a cup of tea in a cafe and asked if we were hungry. I liked him. He was the only person who'd shown any interest in us since we came to London. The old gentleman smiled to us and he said he'd found a room for us, and we could stay there for free. He asked Pete if he wanted to come and look at it first, so Pete went off with him and I stayed near the underground station. I was feeling very tired. My legs had started to swell and I thought I could feel the baby move for the first time. Pete was away for hours and hours. All I could do was sit on a bench outside the cafe and wait. I started to feel nervous. I wasn't sure why exactly."

"When Pete finally came back he looked so strange. Mean and bitter and angry. I'd only seen him look like that once before. It was the night he'd beaten up the tramp up who'd taken our bench. I knew something bad had happened at the old man's house. Pete had a pocket full of money. He said we weren't going to take the room at the old man's house. It was too small, and too dirty. I said I didn't understand. Then he just got angry with me and told me not to ask so many questions. He grabbed my hand and dragged me away from Oxford Street as fast as he could. Pete pulled me so fast I slipped and fell over and tore the skin off my knees. He helped me on to my feet, and almost carried me along. I knew Pete wasn't telling me the truth, but I was too afraid to ask him what had really happened. He never told me and I never asked him about it."

"From that day Pete was a different person. I felt like I didn't know him anymore. Pete started to leave me alone a lot and he only came back to the park at night."

"One weekend Pete didn't come back and I was left alone. It was cold and it rained all the time. Pete came back early on Monday morning and I felt absolutely awful. I had terrible pains inside and a fever. Pete called for an ambulance and I was taken to the nearest hospital. On the way to the hospital I lost consciousness. When I opened my eyes a doctor told me I had lost the baby. It had died because of the infection I had developed. The infection had been caused by cold, damp and being hungry all the time. My body didn't have the strength to fight the infection. I felt like I wanted to die, and Pete had left the hospital when they told him the news. He came back to see me a couple of days later and said how sorry he was and swore that from now on I'd have everything I needed. He swore he would take care of me."

"Four days later I left the hospital and Pete was waiting for me. He took me by taxi to a tiny flat and said it was ours. Then he went away and didn't come back for three more days."

"During the following weeks he was away more than he was at home. I asked him where the money was coming from and he told me he had found a job with a firm that helped people to move house. I still had lots of questions, but I could see I wasn't going to get any more answers from him. Slowly we stopped communicating with each other. He used to talk about the people he worked with and occasionally one of them would come round to our flat to see him. I didn't like them and I was sure he was getting involved in something illegal."

"I was right. One day two policemen came and told me that Pete had been arrested with a gang who specialised in robbing houses. He was in prison. I visited him and he told me to forget all about him and go back to Manchester. He said he wished we had never come down to London. Everything was his fault. Pete felt really sorry for himself. He was unlucky at his trial and met a hard judge who gave him three years. So, now I was all alone and I'd lost everything I cared about."

"At that time I made up my mind that I would never go home and that I would never give up. I swore to myself that I would never be cold or hungry again. All this happened about a year before I met you, Charlie. So you can see I'm used to sleeping out in the open and being cold. I wasn't born holding a bottle of Chanel you know. Charlie, Charlie, are you listening to me?"

Tracey looked down at Charlie and she saw that he was fast asleep. How much had he heard? Tracey moved closer to him and then she too fell asleep.

In the Riverbed

They both felt very cold the next morning. Charlie said he felt a little better, but Tracey didn't believe him. He looked terrible. His face was grey and tired-looking.

Tracey stood up and stretched her tired body. The sun was coming up over the hills. She already knew it was going to be another very hot day. As the morning went by it became hotter and hotter. Tracey took a red lipstick out of her pocket and opened it. She smiled as it ran down her fingers. Her favourite lipstick had melted in the intense heat.

There was no shade down in the dried-up riverbed and not a breath of wind to cool Charlie. The riverbed was probably the absolute hottest place in the whole area. Tracey knew that, unless she could make some kind of shelter for Charlie, he would burn-up. She went down to him and told him she was going to try to move him up to the jeep and put him in the shade.

"You'll never do it, Tracey. I'm too heavy for you."

"I'll do it. I'm tougher than I look. This body is made of steel, Charlie."

"I know, Tracey. I remember most of what you told me about yourself last night."

"Forget what I said last night. Here put this in your mouth."

Tracey handed Charlie a piece of cloth which she'd dipped in water. He looked at it and then at her.

"What's this for?"

"I don't want to hear you screaming when I'm carrying you out of here."

"I won't scream, Tracey."

"Yes you will, now put it in."

Charlie put the gag in his mouth and Tracey bent down and lifted him onto his feet. Charlie's face went red and his eyes bulged out of his head. Tracey let most of his weight rest on the leg that wasn't broken, and then she somehow managed to get him onto her back. Tracey was almost bent double. She felt her legs shaking under his weight. She walked slowly towards a place where she thought it was possible to climb up the riverbank with Charlie on her back. It took a long time, but Tracey finally made it up to the jeep. She sat Charlie down in the shade by the side of the jeep, his back supported by the side of the jeep, as gently as she could. It was difficult because her back felt half-broken and she was exhausted. Tracey took the gag out of Charlie's mouth and he let out a loud, painful groan like a great bull elephant that had just been shot. Tracey poured some water over a silk shirt and wiped his face and his neck. Then, she started to make him a shelter from the burning sun.

It took her most of the morning, but, when she was finished, she was satisfied with her efforts. Tracey had found some dry branches which she'd broken off an old tree and placed them carefully up against the jeep. Then she'd covered the branches with most of the clothes she'd been modelling for the last three days and created a multi-coloured tent that sheltered Charlie from the direct rays of the sun.

"It looks lovely, Tracey. Looks like I won't fry today. That's one of the irritating things about the desert. You fry in the daytime and freeze at night. Can I have some water, please? I'm very thirsty."

Tracey found the giant, plastic water container and carried it over to where Charlie was sitting. She poured him a large cup of water, and, to her horror he gulped it down all at once, smiled, licked his lips and asked for more.

"What's the matter, Tracey?"

"There's not much water left in here, Charlie, and you drink it so fast. We should try to save it."

"Well, just fish out the reserve supply. There's enough in there for almost a week if we're a bit careful. It's in the back of the jeep. I remember filling it up before we left Victoria Springs."

"No, it isn't there, Charlie. I'm sorry, Charlie."

"What are you on about, Tracey? I checked the reserve before we left Victoria Springs. It's the first rule of going out in the desert, make sure you've got extra water. You can last for a long time without food, but you have to have plenty of water. What happened to it, Tracey? Did it get destroyed in the crash?"

Tracey didn't know how to tell him about the water. Now it seemed like she had done an incredibly stupid thing. One little, thoughtless, selfish act, that could cost them their lives.

"I used most of it, Charlie. I'm sorry."

"Say that again, you used it, on what?"

"I've been using it to wash. I felt so dirty and smelly. I needed clean water. I'm sorry, Charlie."

"I just don't believe it, Tracey. You used our

water reserve to wash under your arms and your face? You actually used drinking water for that!"

"I'm sorry, Charlie. I didn't think we'd ever need it. I didn't know you'd crash the jeep."

"So now you're saying it's my fault are you?!"

"No, Charlie. I know it's not your fault. I'm sorry and I'm tired."

"But, Tracey, I made a special stop at the river so you could wash the day before yesterday."

"I know, but the water looked funny and you said there were snakes and crocodiles in it."

"I was just joking!"

"How was I supposed to know that, Charlie? I've never been to Australia before!"

"Great! Wonderful! Now we're certain to die out here, unless we get help fast. You realise what you've done, don't you, Tracey?"

"They'll come out and look for us soon, won't they, Charlie?"

Charlie was silent a moment. He looked away from here.

"What's the matter, Charlie? You did tell the hotel where we were going?"

"I... I didn't say exactly when we were

coming back, and more importantly, we're miles and miles away from the route I said we'd be using. Australia is so huge, Tracey. It could take them weeks to find us and unless we find some water quickly we've had it!"

"I'll find water then, Charlie."

"Where do you think you are, Tracey? Do you expect Tarzan just to appear and carry you off to some beautiful jungle oasis for a cool moonlight swim? There isn't any water out here!"

"I'll... we'll get through this, Charlie. I'm going to the top of the hill. I'll be back as soon as I can."

Tracey gave Charlie some more water and then she said goodbye to him. There was nothing more to say. They had both been foolish and unlucky. Tracey began the long, hard climb up the hillside.

It took her over an hour to reach the top of the hill, and when she arrived she was very tired. From the hilltop she looked in every direction for any sign of human activity. But there was nothing to see. Only mile after mile of rocks, hills and sand. She had the map with her and looked at it. She'd never been very good at reading maps, but she thought she knew in which direction the road lay. It would take her more than a day to reach it, that much was certain. Tracey knew she could never reach it if she had to drag Charlie behind her. She realised that their only chance was for her to go across the country on her own. But she knew she couldn't leave Charlie. He was helpless without her.

When she arrived back at the jeep Charlie was asleep. Flies were busy buzzing around his broken leg. Tracey desperately wanted a drink and she took a small mouthful from the plastic container. It was warm and tasted horrible. She started to gather up some wood for a fire. It was going to be another cold night.

When the bonfire was built Charlie woke up and looked at her.

"I'm sorry I got so angry with you, Tracey. Getting angry and fighting won't help us. We have to stick together. It's our only chance."

"No, I don't think we should stick together, Charlie."

"What do you mean?"

"I think I should go off and try to reach the road. If I travel west all day I'll hit it."

"Don't leave me, Tracey. I don't want to be left on my own out here."

"We have to find water, or help, Charlie."

"How will you find your way around out there? You don't know the desert. The light is funny and plays tricks on your mind. It's hard to judge distances properly. It's dangerous trying to walk across the desert."

"I've got the map."

"Tracey, that map is no good for walking. It shows where roads are and rivers and mountains, but there's not enough information on it. You'll get lost."

"Have you got a better idea? We don't have any choice."

"I saw some kind of wild dog down in the riverbed, Tracey. It was digging for water. There's water down there. We could try and dig too."

"I'll have to do all the digging, Charlie, and I'm tired."

"Don't go, Tracey. Try digging for water first, please?"

Tracey gave Charlie some more painkillers from the first aid box. Then she took the shovel from the jeep and climbed down into the riverbed and started to dig. If Charlie wanted her to dig, she would dig and maybe he was right. Perhaps she would find water down there.

After half an hour she was more than four feet down and the earth began to change colour and get darker. She got down on her hands and knees and felt the earth in her fingers. It was damp.

Tracey kept on digging. Her back hurt and she was getting blisters on her hands, but still she kept on digging. It was very hot in the hole and her whole body was dripping with sweat. Her shirt and jeans were soaking wet and her hair was sticking to her neck and face. At the end of an hour there was still no real sign of water, and, finally, Tracey dropped the shovel and began digging hysterically with her hands in the damp earth. She filled her mouth with a handful of earth and then spat it out.

It was then she realised that the hole she had been digging was probably her own grave, and she had wasted her energy on nothing at all. It was total madness. Tracey was so angry with herself. She dragged herself out of the hole, back up the side of the riverbed and crawled back into the shelter she had built next to the jeep. Tracey took just a mouthful of water and then she fell asleep.

When she opened her eyes the air felt cooler and the sun was sinking. She looked up at

Charlie and he smiled at her.

"I've been watching you sleeping. You look nice when you're asleep. I should have taken some photographs of you when you were asleep."

"You can take some of me when we get back to civilisation."

Charlie was silent for a few moments. Then he looked at Tracey again and said:

"Listen to me, Tracey. I've been thinking. I want you to get out of here, tonight. Go before it's too late."

"I don't want to leave you, Charlie. You need me."

"There's no water here, Tracey, and I can't go with you. You have got to go and find some, for me and for yourself."

"I don't want to go!"

"This is your chance, Tracey. Go ahead and take it!"

Charlie looked away from her and out over the endless desert. He was sitting staring into space and he looked like he was seeing something that wasn't really there.

"The first time I saw you was in the King's Road in Chelsea. Do you remember? It was a beautiful spring day and the flowers were blooming. You were standing outside a boutique and there was a crowd of Japanese tourists all around you. You were letting them take pictures of you for money. I was just out for a walk. I noticed the way you posed for all those people. I thought you had a good face and you were tall enough. You had... you had something I liked, raw talent. I'm good at spotting talent. Do you remember?"

"I was too thin and my arms and legs were too long. I looked like a spider wearing too much make-up."

"I know that, but you had your own style and that comes from the inside. There are lots of pretty young girls around. Only I thought you had a special expression in your eyes and you knew instinctively how to move your body. That made me notice you. Later on I found out that you looked good in anything. Some people are lucky that way. God gave you something special, Tracey."

Tracey remembered how exciting it had been at the beginning. Modelling was the first real job she'd ever had and she enjoyed it. It was fun to wear nice clothes and make herself look beautiful. She started to earn money and moved into a little flat in Notting Hill Gate.

She looked up at the clear desert sky.

"I wish it would rain, Charlie."

"Tracey, take half the water and leave me. The sun's going down now. If you keep moving all night you can travel a long way. As soon as the sun comes up tomorrow morning, stop and find some shade. Sleep all day. Then when it gets dark again carry on moving. You'll reach the main road and then bring back help. I'll be fine on my own. I want you to go and get help, Tracey."

"I'm not stupid, Charlie. You want to be noble and heroic."

"I'm trying to be realistic, Tracey. There is no reason why we both have to... have to wait here."

"Let me think, Charlie."

"There's nothing to think about. Start the fire and gather some more wood and then get out of here, understood!"

Tracey knew that Charlie was right. She crawled out of the shelter and began to gather more dry wood for the fire. Then she filled a small plastic bottle with water for her journey.

"Goodbye, Charlie."

"Say 'see you soon'."

"See you soon, Charlie. I've always liked you, you know. I wouldn't have got anywhere without your help."

"Yes, you would, Tracey. Someone else would eventually have seen your potential."

"I'll be back as soon as I can."

"I know you will, Tracey. I know you will. Good luck, beautiful."

Aborigines

Tracey climbed back up to the track and moved off in the direction of the road. She was nervous and a little bit scared. What would happen when she got to the road? When they'd been on it they hadn't seen a car all day. Tracey walked and walked and the track went on and on.

She was pleased when the sun went down and the darkness finally fell. Tracey looked at the map with her torch and calculated that Victoria Springs was almost two hundred kilometres away. Could she really walk two hundred kilometres across the desert? Of course not. It was impossible. Impossible, but she could find herself forced to try it.

All sorts of strange thoughts began to run through her head. She started to think of Paris, Milan and Tokyo. About walking up and down the catwalk in front of hundreds of photographers. About all the amazingly expensive clothes she'd worn. Beautiful, wonderful, marvelous clothes. Now, all that world seemed like something from a dream. She'd loved it all in the beginning. Tracey had entered a different world and enjoyed it. It was hard work, but, compared to living on the street, it was paradise. For the first time in her life she had found something she was good at. Her face appeared on the cover of fashion magazines and people began to recognise her.

She had been lucky that Charlie had spotted her in the King's Road and had given her a chance in front of a camera. But she had also worked very hard. She was always ready and willing to work, and she was always friendly and smiling. Also her face just seemed to look right. She had big eyes, a small nose and a large mouth with full lips. When she started she was almost seventeen, but, luckily, she looked three years younger. Top models were getting younger and younger all the time.

Then she had another piece of luck. Tracey met a famous Italian film director who liked her and put her in a television video for a new Fiat car. She was paid ten thousand pounds for just a week's work.

Tracey kept on thinking and she kept on walking. She looked at her watch and saw that she'd been walking for a long time. Somehow the track had disappeared. She was standing in the desert, and she had no idea where she was. Tracey looked at the map again. It didn't help very much. Tracey thought she was walking in the right direction, but she was not absolutely sure. She thought about trying to find her way back to Charlie. Could she find her way back?

Tracey began to realise that she was probably lost. Would somebody find her someday and think she was a dry, withered Egyptian mummy? Would there be anything left of her famous face and body at all? A terrible feeling of horror and panic began to race through her body. It started down in the pit of her stomach and spread. Tracey stopped walking and wrapped her arms around her body. She felt cold and she was shivering. It suddenly hit her that she was all alone, and the nearest town was hundreds of kilometres away.

Tracey looked up at the stars above her head. The air was so clear in the desert and she had never seen stars that looked so big or so bright. Tracey saw a star shooting across the sky. She wondered if her life was like that star. To die out here on her own was unfair. She had at least fifty or sixty years of normal life left. She opened her beautiful, wide mouth and scream-

ed in protest up at the stars. Tracey felt the air rushing out of her lungs and her voice echo around her in the endless darkness. She felt tired and helpless and stupid. There was no one to hear her or help her, and she felt closer and closer to madness.

"What are you shouting for? The stars won't help you if you scream at them. That's not the way to call for help from heaven."

Tracey had heard the deep voice behind her, but she didn't believe it was real. Still, she turned around and switched on her torch. She almost collapsed when she saw three dark figures standing only about ten feet away from her.

The three Aborigines were almost naked and carrying spears. They had thick, curly hair and they had paint on their bodies. The man standing closest to her, was also the youngest. He smiled at her and spoke again. This time there was no humour in his voice.

"What are you doing out here? Have you had an accident? Are you in trouble?"

"Yes... yes. I'm in trouble. There's been an accident. My friend is badly hurt. His leg is smashed. Our jeep went off the road and plunged down a hillside. He's back there in an old riverbed. Please help him. I think he's dying."

The young man at the front turned to his two companions and said something to them. Then they disappeared into the darkness. He then came closer to Tracey and handed her a kind of round wooden bottle. He told her to drink and she drank. It tasted strange, but it was liquid and that was the most important thing.

"I know it doesn't taste like Coke, but it's a lot better for your teeth and it'll help your throat and give you strength. My two mates will go along the river and find your friend. It won't take them long. They know this whole area well."

"But I've been walking for hours and hours. He's miles and miles away."

"Your friend isn't very far away. You see, I think you've been walking around in a big circle for a long time. You were trying to reach the road to Victoria Springs, weren't you?"

"Yes, I was trying to reach the road."

"Well, you're not going in the right direction."

"What... what are you doing out here?"

"I came out to find you."

"You're part of the search party, are you?"

"No, there's no search party, as far as I know."

"I don't understand. You said you came looking for me."

"I... I saw you in a dream. A tall white woman with dark hair going around and around in a big circle."

"You saw me in a dream?"

"Look, I don't expect you to understand. That isn't really important now. The important thing is I'm here and you are safe."

"I still don't understand you. I'm glad you're here and all that, but what are you talking about?"

"Come with me and have some food. When you feel better we can have a talk about it, if you still want to."

See Forever

A large, mysterious rock formation rose out of the desert in front of them. As they came nearer the Aborigine camp the moon came out from behind the clouds and gave Tracey a clear view. It was at the foot of the rocks. The rocks reflected the moonlight and looked a strange colour in the darkness. There were about ten or fifteen shacks in the camp. They were not very pretty to look at. The Aborigines had used anything they could find to make them. Old wooden boxes, the doors and bonnets from cars, metal sheets, plastic sheets and all sorts of other things. There were old, rusty cars lying around all over the place. Tracey found it hard to believe that people lived in these shacks.

The young man said his name was Paul and he opened the door to one of the shacks. Tracey followed him inside. There was an old woman sleeping in one corner and two small children next to her.

"That's my granny Dora. You can sleep over there. I'll get you a blanket to keep you warm and something to eat and drink. I'll be back in a minute."

"Can't you telephone for a helicopter and some help. My friend Charlie needs a doctor quickly."

"First, we don't have a telephone or a radio, second the nearest doctor is three hundred kilometres away. Don't worry about your friend, we'll do everything we can for him. As soon as he arrives my granny will take a look at him."

Then he smiled at her and left the shack. A few minutes later he returned with the food, a bottle of water and a blanket.

"I've sent two more men to help with your friend. They'll be back soon. Now, eat and drink and get some sleep."

Tracey ate the meat and drank the water. Nothing had ever tasted as good as this food. She smiled and felt a lot better. The young man put the blanket around her shoulders and sat down next to her.

"Tell me the truth," said Tracey. "How did you find me?"

"I told you the truth, now, lie down and go to sleep. Tomorrow there will be time to talk."

Then he stood up and left the shack. Suddenly Tracey felt incredibly tired. She lat down on her mat, pulled the blanket up around her ears and closed her heavy eyes. A few seconds later she was asleep.

The next morning when Tracey woke up, she opened her eyes and looked around the hut. It was empty, beams of sunlight were streaming through the holes in the roof.

Tracey stood up and wrapped the coloured cotton blanket around herself and went out into the sunlight. A group of about ten Aborigines were sitting crossed-legged in a circle talking. As she came closer they all turned and looked at her and smiled. She recognised Paul who came over to her. He told her that his four friends had brought Charlie to the camp safely and that his granny had already had a look at Charlie's leg. Charlie was not going to die.

"That's great, can I see him?"

"My granny gave him something to make him sleep, but as soon as he wakes up you can talk to him."

"I didn't get to say 'thank you' last night, Paul. If you hadn't found us we would have died for sure. By the way, my name's Tracey."

"You don't need to thank me. Do you fancy a little walk, or do you want breakfast straightaway, Tracey?"

"I'm not really hungry and it's a wonderful

morning. Let's walk."

They walked towards the rocks behind the camp. The rocks were further away than Tracey had thought. Charlie was right, it was difficult to judge distances in the desert.

"The air's so clear out here, Paul."

"It's because there are no factories out here in the desert. But if you go in a straight line in that direction," said Paul pointing to the left, "then you end up in the old nuclear testing area they used years ago. The whole area is covered in radioactive hotspots. It's best to keep away."

"Don't worry. I'm not planning to go there."

"You know, Tracey. It doesn't matter where you go on this planet. There is no way to escape the white man's civilisation. In the end, you destroy everything you touch."

"I thought I was going to die yesterday, Paul. I really felt like I was face to face with death. From now on every day will feel like a gift, an bonus."

"That's good. I hope you remember how you feel today. Remember how wonderful life is and don't waste it."

"I'll do my best, Paul."

Paul smiled at Tracey and they arrived at the foot of the rocks a short time later.

There was a narrow path between the rocks and Tracey followed it upwards. After about ten minutes' climbing they reached a flat area in front of a large, dark cave. Paul sat down on a rock near the entrance. Tracey sat beside him. The rock was so smooth and Tracey asked him how that could be. Paul answered that the rock was smooth because so many people had sat on it. Tracey looked out over the desert. She felt like she could see forever. Then she looked down at the scruffy huts below.

"I know the camp isn't very pretty. In fact it's horrible, ugly. We plan to clear it up later. We're just beginning, you see."

"What are you beginning, Paul?"

"A new start."

"Have you always lived here?"

"No, my parents moved to Sydney before I was born. My father had heard a lot about the city and he went to have a look for himself. In those days lots of our people were fascinated by the big city. I went to a white school and learnt lots of useless stuff about England and Europe. I didn't like going to school very much, but I'm not stupid, Tracey. I just didn't fit in."

"I can hear you're not stupid, Paul. What happened after school?"

"After school I had lots of low-paid, dead-end jobs. But I'm not complaining. I didn't have any qualifications. It wasn't a very good time for me, Tracey. I started drinking heavily. Alcohol is a huge problem for my people. It's the whiteman's secret weapon.

Anyway, one morning I woke up on the beach, bloody, beaten and naked. I should have been dead, but I wasn't. I looked over the ocean towards the sun. It's sounds crazy. I heard this voice calling me by name. The voice told me to clean up and go home where I belonged."

"Wow!"

"I know it sounds strange, Tracey, but the words went right to the centre of my soul. I stood up, threw my bottle into the water, turned around and began to walk home. It took me a couple of months, but when I came here, I knew I had arrived. This was the right place to start all over again."

Tracey looked over her shoulder towards the mouth of the cave and then back towards Paul.

"Are you going to stay here? Are you never going to go back to the city?"

"No, I'm never going back to the city. There's nothing in the city I want. Here I'm learning about the ways of our people. Our people have so much knowledge. What I want to do is find my roots again."

"Sometimes I feel like I don't have any roots. I pulled up my roots years ago. I'm a model and I'm always traveling. I don't have time to grow roots. Roots slow you down."

Then Paul said something that surprised Tracey.

"Are you happy with your life, Tracey?"

"Of course I'm happy. I've got everything I ever dreamed of having. I've got money. A flat in London. A nice car. I know lots of great people."

"That's good. In my dream about you I had the feeling that you were unhappy."

"No, I'm not unhappy. I'm just a little bit tired. I've been working hard for years. Maybe I need a holiday. Maybe I need a rest from modelling. Sometimes I get sick of the sight of my own face looking back at me from magazines."

They sat in silence for a few minutes.

"What are you thinking about, Tracey?"

"Don't you ever feel very small out here? I mean the desert is so enormous."

"I used to feel very small. Then I realised that I was part of something much, much bigger than me. I'm part of all this. We all can be part of nature, if we want to."

"I don't feel like I'm part of nature, Paul."

"You will do eventually, Tracey. All you white people will have to learn that again. You can't fight nature forever. Your world is slowly falling apart."

Tracey didn't know how to reply to this, so she tried to change the subject.

"How long have your people been in Australia, Paul?"

"My people have been here in Australia for about a hundred thousand years. For tens of thousands of years we lived in perfect harmony and balance with nature. We know a lot about nature. We have an old and very sophisticated culture."

"It doesn't look very 'sophisticated', Paul." Tracey pointed at the scruffy camp below them.

"That's because our culture isn't based on materialism like yours is. Your God is money. What we really value is wisdom and knowledge, not wealth and things. Did you know we have the oldest stories in the world? They've been handed down from generation to generation. Stories that are twenty, thirty, forty thousand years old. They're important stories.

We understood this planet, nature and the universe thousands of years before the pyramids or your cities were built. I've started to learn about so many amazing things here. You white people travel into space in rockets and think you've made fantastic progress. But I know an old man who travels through space and time using his mind. He travels faster than the speed of light. He's visited other worlds and planets!"

"And do you believe him, Paul?"

"I believe in God and God can do anything. It's like I told you, we've had tens of thousands of years to explore our minds. There is more inside us than you people understand. You think you know everything, but you don't. You're only just beginning to ask the right questions. I hope it's not too late for you."

"Charlie said living out in the desert changes people."

"It's true, Moses and Jesus and Mohammed all came out of the desert. The desert is a good place to think. A good place to meet God."

Paul smiled and looked over his shoulder towards the cave.

"Listen to me, Tracey. Come with me into that cave behind us."

"What for, what's in there?"

"It's one of the oldest places in this whole country. It's a very special place for my people, a holy place. A secret place. We've used it for thousands of years in our ceremonies. There are painted symbols on the walls and there are signs cut into the rocks. I can help you read and understand, Tracey. There are secrets which will take your breath away. I can help you open your mind and find another reality beyond this one."

"Ummm... thanks, Paul, but I... I don't really want to go in there. This all seems like a dream to me. In a minute I'll wake up and I'll be in my bed in Victoria Springs."

"You're right, Tracey. You have been 'dreaming'. Your whole life has been a kind of dream. Now, for the first time, you have a chance to wake up and open your eyes."

"Thanks a lot, Paul. I know you mean well and you believe what you say, only... only I'm not ready to go into that cave right now. I don't think I'll ever want to go in there. Listen, I have to get Charlie back, and I have to be in Sydney in a few days. I've got so much work to do. I've got a life, but thanks for asking me."

"Are you sure, Tracey?"

"Ahhh... yes, thanks, but no thanks."

"Come back here, if you feel like it, Tracey. We'll be waiting. These rocks aren't going anywhere. We've got all the time in the world."

"Ummm... yes I'll give you a call next time I'm in Australia. Now I think it's time I went down and saw how Charlie is getting on. He'll think I've run out on him again."

Tracey stood up and began to walk down the narrow path between the rocks. When she reached the ground she turned and looked back. Paul was standing with his arms outstretched on either side of him forming a cross. She wondered for a second if what he had told her about the cave was really true. Did Paul truly believe that a man could travel through time and space and visit other worlds? No, it was too fantastic. They had all been out in the hot sun too long. Tracey decided to get back to the 'real world' as fast as possible. She walked over to the camp and asked where Charlie was.

Trouble Smiling

Tracey entered the hut were Charlie was sleeping. She knelt down beside him and watched him. His face looked peaceful and most of the colour had come back. She put her hand on his forehead and his temperature felt normal. Charlie opened his eyes and smiled at her.

"Hello, Charlie. I'm sorry if I woke you."

"Hello, Tracey. Where are we? Why am I still alive?"

"It's a bit of a strange story..."

When she'd told Charlie everything, he still looked a bit puzzled.

"Have they sent someone to Victoria Springs to bring back help?"

"Yes, but it will take some for them to walk there."

"Walk there? This is crazy. We're arrived back in the Stone Age with these people."

"Charlie, four of these people carried you out of the valley and brought you here last night. We owe these people our lives. They may not be just like us, but we still have to show them some respect."

"I'm sorry, Tracey. You're right. It's just hard to imagine anyone living without a telephone and a television in the modern world."

"They aren't living in the modern world anymore, Charlie. They've left it behind them."

"Well, this has certainly been an interesting trip into the desert."

"Yeah, a real adventure. I hope I never have to go through anything like it again for the rest of my life."

A couple of days later, two large, four-wheel-drive jeeps arrived from Victoria Springs. There was a doctor in one of the off-roaders and he examined Charlie. He gave him some antibiotics and a shot of morphine. The doctor waited for the painkiller to work, then he cleaned up Charlie's broken leg and had him carried to one of the off-roaders.

Tracey and Charlie then said goodbye and thanked Paul and the others for everything they had done for them. As they drove away across the desert toward the road, Tracey saw that Paul was standing waving goodbye to her on his own. She watched him getting smaller and smaller as they drove away. Finally he was just a tiny dot, then he vanished. Tracey was sure she would never see him, or the rocks or the mysterious cave again.

About two hours later they reached the road to Victoria Springs, and, by mid-afternoon, they were back in the small town they had left several days earlier. Tracey felt like she had been away for years.

Everything looked the same, but at the same time everything looked different. She couldn't figure out how things had changed. Then she realised that everything was the same. Nothing had really changed in Victoria Springs at all. It was she who had changed. And the worst part of it was that she wasn't sure how or why it had happened to her.

The next morning a small plane flew them to the nearest big town. From there they caught a large passenger plane to Sydney. When Tracey looked out of the window and down at the city she had a shock. There were so many buildings and so many roads. The plane descended and she could see all the people. The desert had been so peaceful and empty and now, suddenly, she was back in the noisy city surrounded by people.

There was a group of journalists and cameramen who had discovered what had happened to her out in the endless wilderness. Tracey suddenly realised that she hadn't combed her hair for days or put on her makeup. Charlie was taken from the airport to a private clinic. He had a nice room with a big window overlooking over the ocean.

"What are you going to do now, Tracey?" Charlie asked her.

"I've got to get back to London. I telephoned my agent a few hours ago and she said to fly back as soon as possible."

"Are you still with Linda Whitehouse?"

"Yes."

"I used to know her a long time ago. Is she treating you all right?"

"She's clever and she's made me lots of money. Linda is a great agent."

"She's also made a lot of money for herself."

"I'm not complaining about what Linda does. She's helped me a lot, Charlie."

"She made you pull some teeth out, didn't she."

"It was only four wisdom teeth, Charlie. Without them my face looked thinner. I thought it was a good idea. It improved my face."

"What about that little bit of work on your nose? What about the silicone injections in your lips and breasts? That silicone stuff can move around the body, you know. It's probably dangerous."

"Charlie, sometimes nature needs a helping hand. Linda's clients want perfect girls and I agreed to some improvement work. Anyway, I don't want to think about it now. I'm flying back to London tonight. I hope you get well soon. Can you pay the bills here? Do you need some money?"

"No, Tracey. I can pay my own hospital bills. Have a good time back in London. Maybe you should have a holiday or a rest after all that's happened."

"I've had a holiday, Charlie. A wonderful week in the great Australian desert!"

"I'm sorry, Tracey. It was all my fault. I was stupid to go out there alone with you."

"It wasn't your fault, Charlie. I wanted to go with you. I thought it would be fun just to get away from the world for a few days."

"I won't forget what you did for me back in the desert. You saved my life."

"We both had our lives saved by the Aborigines."

"I still remember the things you told me about yourself. The way you used to live on the streets. You never told me anything about any of that before."

"I didn't think it was important. I wanted to forget about being poor and enjoy my life. Listen, Charlie, I don't want you to go around and tell everybody. I've got a good chance of getting a perfume contract. They are talking about half a million over four years. Linda wants me to develop a more 'sophisticated' image. The perfume people want a 'young lady'."

"Don't worry, Tracey. I can keep my mouth shut. Whatever happened to that boy you were with on the streets? The one who went to prison?"

"His name was Pete. I heard later that he was out of prison and had moved back to Manchester. I don't know anything else. Sometimes I... sometimes I think..."

"What do you think?"

"I've been thinking about going back to Manchester and visiting my parents. I haven't seen them for years."

"I think I know what your trouble is, Tracey."

"What's my trouble, Charlie? I feel fine."

"I think you're getting tired of all this. I can see it in your face and your eyes. I notice things. You need a rest. When was the last time you had a holiday?"

"I had a week-end off six months ago."

"Listen, I still care about you a lot, Tracey. If you change your mind about us, come back to Australia. I'll always be here for you if you need me. We could work together, maybe?"

"Doing what, Charlie?"

"I don't know, Tracey. We'd think of something. There are lots of possibilities in Australia."

"Thanks, Charlie, I'll keep it in mind."

"I'll wait for you, Tracey."

"I know, Charlie. It's nice to know I've got one good friend."

Tracey kissed Charlie and went over to the door. Before she left she turned, and smiled at him, and said.

"Take care of yourself, Charlie. It was nice to see you again. And if you ever want me to do you a favour again or go out into the desert, don't call me – ask someone else."

London Again

Linda Whitehouse's office was at the top of a beautiful modern building down by the River Thames. It was surrounded by other modern buildings, buildings that would still look good in two hundred years. The large entrance to the building was full of light and exotic plants and expensive Italian marble. Tracey told the security guards her name and that she had an appointment with Linda. One of the big guards escorted her over to the lift and pressed the button for her. He waited until she was inside and then went back to the desk near the entrance. The lift went right to the top of the building and Tracey stepped out into a large, luxurious office.

The whole place was full of incredibly attractive young women and men. They all had beautiful clothes and perfect hair. Everyone seemed to have soaked themselves in perfume and aftershave and expensive body lotions. All the different colours and smells were almost overpowering. Tracey remembered the desert and how 'pure' everything had been there.

It was stupid, but suddenly she began to feel old. The young people in the office were four or five years younger than she was and they looked so fresh and enthusiastic about everything. They looked so hopeful. She knew that lots of young people dreamt about a career in modelling. How many of them would make it? One in every thousand, maybe. How many of them realised how hard the job was? None of them looked at Tracey who wasn't wearing any make-up, but only a pair of old jeans and a checked shirt.

Linda smiled warmly as Tracey entered her spacious office.

"How do you like my new office? I got so tired of all that old stuff I had in here. Do you like the new furniture? I got that Japanese guy Akiro to do everything. I think this room is just wonderful, don't you?"

"Yes, it's very nice, Linda."

"You know they spent almost a million pounds on the marble downstairs at the entrance and then the bank who own the building said the colour didn't feel right, so they spent another million putting new marble in. Amazing, isn't it?"

"I'm impressed."

"I read all about your adventure in the desert. Did it really happen like they say in the newspapers?"

"It wasn't an 'adventure', Linda. It was real."

"Yes, it was 'real', wasn't it. I really think we need more of that in our lives – reality. Things that are one hundred percent authentic."

"What are you talking about, Linda?"

"I'm talking about reality. You've seen reality. Not like the rest of us who protected all the time, surrounded by civilisation. You're lucky, Tracey."

"I was close to death, Linda. I didn't enjoy it. I'm lucky to be alive."

"Somebody should take some photographs of you now, Tracey. Without any make-up. You look so real! When people see your face and the clothes you're wearing they'll think of 'reality' and 'authenticity'. Those are very important qualities. People pay for 'quality'. Do you remember how Benetton used 'reality' in their campaigns?"

"Linda, I'm just tired. I don't feel like selling my face today."

"What a shame. It would be a good career move for you, Tracey. A very good move. What I mean is you're not getting any younger, are you?"

Tracey thought this was a strange thing for Linda to say, but before she had the chance to say anything, one of the four telephones on Linda's desk began to buzz. Linda picked it up and began to talk to someone in California.

All the time Tracey could see from the expression on Linda's face that she had something important to say to her, only she didn't know how to begin. This was also a surprise to Tracey, as Linda always seemed to know what to say.

Tracey knew that Linda had been in the business for years and years. She didn't know how Linda kept looking so beautiful year after year. There were lots of rumours about how Linda kept so young-looking. It was said that she had spent a small fortune on plastic surgery at specialist clinics in Miami, Los Angeles and Switzerland. Tracey sat looking at Linda's beautiful, smiling face. She watched the perfect lips moving and stopped listening to what Linda was saying.

Tracey began to think about how much of Linda was real and how much was false, and did 'real' and `false' have any meaning anymore? Was it wrong to use your money to make yourself more beautiful? Why not buy a better nose, better cheekbones, remove the lines around the eyes. But Tracey knew that Linda had always been beautiful. Linda didn't need to improve or help nature.

And suddenly Tracey understood what Linda was doing. Linda was trying to stop time, she was trying to stop herself growing old.

Linda put the telephone down and began to talk to Tracey, but Tracey wasn't listening. She was thinking about time. You couldn't stop time, no matter how much money you spent. Tracey knew that she wasn't afraid of growing old. She couldn't stay young forever, and she didn't care. She knew that she had a brain, a heart, and it didn't matter what they looked like as long as they worked properly.

Tracey knew that she didn't want to fight time. It was a stupid battle that nobody could win. She kept on looking at Linda's face and nothing else seemed to exist in the whole world, only Linda's face.

Tracey suddenly remembered something important. Paul had said it to her on their way down from the cave. She could hear his voice clearly once more. He had said: '...Always remember, Tracey, there is more of you on the inside than there is on the outside.' Tracey hadn't really understood what he'd meant by this, but now, suddenly, she did.

"Tracey, are you listening to me?" Linda sounded very irritated, Tracey knew she hated it when people didn't listen to her properly.

"Oh, sorry, Linda. I was just day-dreaming about Australia, sorry."

"The Australian press is sending an army of journalists out to find that Aborigine camp in the desert."

"It's not true?"

"The story is front page news in Australia, Tracey."

"Can't we stop them, Linda?"

"It's too late for that. You know what happens when they sniff out a good story: 'Supermodel's Desert Drama', 'Naked in the Sun'."

"The Aborigines will hate it. They just want to be left alone."

"I understand, Tracey. Here's what I think we should do. In a few days you should fly back to Australia and visit their camp. You could take along some presents for them. Medicine, clothes, maybe a radio or even a television. They have electricity, don't they? How does that sound to you? It would be good for you at this stage in your career."

"No! I won't do it, Linda. Those people don't want anything from us, that's why they've gone back to the desert."

"All right, all right, Tracey. You don't have to go back if you don't want to. But you can't stop the Australian newspapers doing whatever they want."

"This isn't what I wanted to happen. I owe those people everything. They saved my life."

"All right, I can understand that, Tracey." Linda looked nervous, and this was unusual.

"What's the matter with you, Linda? What plans have you got up your sleeve for me now?"

"Tracey, you know I've always really liked you a lot. I think of you almost like a younger sister. I always try to get to know my girls, but, with you, it's been different. You were always so mysterious about your past."

"That's because I was only interested in the future, Linda. There was nothing worth remembering in the past."

"Ahh, the future. Your future. Sometimes... sometimes I wish I could stop time. Nothing lasts for ever, Tracey."

"I know, Linda."

"I've had an offer from an American publisher, Tracey. They want you to be in a book."

"What kind of book? It sounds interesting."

"You remember that book Madonna did a few years ago?"

"The one where she stripped naked?"

"Yeah, that's the one. It sold millions. I've talked to the photographers and they've got some great ideas for what they want to do with you. Your book will make Madonna look like a nun."

"You mean I'll have to take all my clothes off in front of the whole world?"

"They are willing to pay you almost five hundred thousand pounds. That's a lot of money for taking your clothes off. I mean you did stuff like it before, when you started out in the business."

"I was 'hungry' then, Linda."

"I know you were, Tracey. You were the most ambitious girl I'd ever met."

"I don't understand, Linda. I thought we were developing a 'sophisticated' image for me. What happened to that and the perfume deal?"

Linda was silent for a few seconds, but to Tracey it felt like years.

"The truth is this, Tracey. You're too old, and your face isn't fashionable anymore. Well, it won't be in six months time. Your face is out of date."

"I'm only twenty-four, Linda!"

"I've got girls on my books who are thirteen. Their mothers drag them here. You've had a great ride, Tracey, and now it's somebody else's turn. Things happen fast in this business these days. There are a thousand girls waiting to take your place and they'll do anything we ask them. They are still 'hungry', Tracey."

"You mean I'm finished. Is that what you mean, Linda?"

"You're not finished, Tracey. Only this is the top of the ladder for you. I don't think you're going to climb any higher. Now the only way is down. You can go down slowly, and still make some money, or you can go down fast. It's up to you."

"Thanks a lot, Linda!"

"I don't want to lie to you, Tracey. Do this book while you've still got a good body. In a few years nobody will ask you to do a book. Don't turn down all that money. Don't be stupid. Make some money while you've still got something to sell!"

"Linda, I don't want to do it."

"Why not? When you're an old woman you can show people the book and let them see what you looked like when you were young and had a perfect body."

"Give me a few days to think about it, Linda."

"All right, but don't take too long about it. I've a room-full of 'hungry' girls out there."

Linda pressed a button on her desk and her secretary came in. He was very handsome and Tracey hadn't seen him before. Linda asked him to bring Lucy in.

Tracey stood up, said goodbye and promised she'd telephone Linda as soon as she'd made up her mind about the book. On her way out Tracey met Lucy coming in. Lucy was very tall, with long straight hair, enormous, green eyes, a small nose and a wide mouth. Lucy looked like she was about fifteen. Lucy looked 'hungry'.

When Tracey arrived back at her flat there were journalists and photographers waiting for her. She told the taxi driver to keep on driving. She crawled down on to the floor so nobody would see her as they drove past.

Later she hired a car and drove out of London on the motorway heading west. As she drove she kept looking behind her in the mirror to see if she was being followed.

Water Under the Bridge

Tracey was glad when London disappeared behind her. Soon there was countryside around her. There were low, rolling hills, trees and rich, green fields. She left the motorway and drove along narrow, winding country roads. Then she started to drive north and she drove all day without a break. She suddenly knew where she was going, but she really didn't know why.

At about five o'clock in the afternoon she had reached the outskirts of Manchester, the city where she had been born. She had sworn to herself that she would never return to Manchester, but now she was back again.

The city seemed to have changed a lot. There were lots of new roads everywhere and Tracey realised that she was lost. It seemed stupid to be lost in her own home town!

She stopped the car, got out to stretch her legs and look at the map. A young policeman came over to her and asked her if she needed any help. Tracey explained that she hadn't been in Manchester for a long time and everything looked different.

"You don't want to go to that part of the city, Miss. If you go there in that smart car, you'll have to walk home."

"What do you mean?"

"Moss Side is a bad area. There's a lot of crime there and it's got worse over the last five years. Don't go there unless you really have to, Miss."

"I really do have to go there. That's where my Mum and Dad live."

The young policeman then told Tracey to be careful and gave her instructions how to get there.

Tracey arrived in Moss Side after crossing the city. The area had changed, that much was clear. It looked poorer and lots of the shops were shut. There were groups of young men on the street corners and they looked at her suspiciously as she drove by.

Finally Tracey arrived at the block of flats where her parents lived. She parked the car and locked it carefully. The lift in the flats

JOHNSON. H.
SMITH

didn't work so Tracey climbed up the stairs, all the way to the top. Tracey wondered what her parents would say when she knocked on the door.

She walked down the corridor to their flat and knocked on the blue door. Her mother opened it and looked up at Tracey. She put her hand up to her mouth, and then took it away and called over her shoulder,

"Bill, it's Tracey, she's come home!"

Tracey heard her father say something, but she couldn't understand what it was. Her mother wiped a tear from the corner of her eye and pulled Tracey inside the little flat.

Her father was sitting in the same armchair where he always sat. There was a little table beside him. It had a transistor radio on it, a cup of tea, and, most important of all, the newspaper open at the television page. He looked up at her and smiled.

"You look different, Tracey. Your face is different," he said.

"I'm just older, Dad. How are you?"

"I'm fine, Tracey. You've got a good colour."

"Thanks. Dad. I've been in Australia."

"I know I read about the trouble you had in the desert. You should be careful where you go."

"I know, Dad."

"You take your clothes off a lot, Tracey. I've seen your picture in the paper hundreds of times, stark naked!"

"It's my job, Dad. It doesn't mean anything. You get used to it after a time."

"Are you getting on all right with your job?"

"It's not too bad, Dad. I earn a fortune."

"You earn a fortune for taking your clothes off?"

"Yeah, sometimes I do. I don't take them off so much now."

"That's good. I'm not stupid you know, Tracey. Why did you come back here? Is anything wrong? Can we help?"

"I'm all right, Dad, honest."

"Mmm... I don't know. Are you sure you're happy, Tracey?"

Tracey thought for a moment. Charlie, Paul and now her Dad. All of them had asked her if she was happy. Did she really look so unhappy?

"I'm... I'm getting a bit bored with it. I'm having trouble smiling."

Tracey was surprised when her father burst out laughing at this.

"What's the matter, Dad?"

"It's what you said about having trouble smiling. Everybody around this area has trouble smiling these days, and they don't have a good job like you do."

Tracey's dad turned to Tracey's mum and asked her to put the kettle on for a fresh cup of tea. Tracey followed her mum out into the tiny kitchen.

"He's really pleased to see you, Tracey."

"Is he, Mum?"

"He's got an album with all your pictures from the newspaper in it."

"Really?"

"How long are you staying with us, Tracey?"

"I don't know for sure, Mum. I'm having a little break from modelling."

They took the tea back to the sitting room and they sat together and talked about what Tracey had been doing and how much Moss Side had changed. Then there was a knock on the door.

"I wonder who that can be?" Tracey's mum said and left them. She came back with a young man who was carrying two plastic buckets.

"Hello, Ted," said Tracey's dad and he introduced Ted to Tracey. "Ted lives two floors down, Tracey. He's come to borrow some water. Can you help him carry one of the buckets back downstairs, Tracey?"

"Yeah, of course I can." Tracey answered and followed Ted out into the kitchen. Ted gave Tracey a shy smile but he didn't say anything. She helped him down the stairs with the heavy buckets.

Ted opened the door to his flat and they went inside.

"They cut my water off because I couldn't pay the bill. So now we have to borrow water from the neighbours," Ted said.

He went out into the bathroom with the bucket and Tracey put her's on the kitchen table. There was a terrible smell in the kitchen. A squadron of fat, black flies were circling around the light bulb. The naked light bulb reminded Tracey of the hot desert sun. The circling flies made her think about the buzzards she had seen there. Like enormous, monstrous flies, the buzzards scanned the desert far below, searching for anything that was dead.

Tracey shivered and rubbed her hands together for warmth. She suddenly understood how close she had been to becoming just 'dead meat'. Maybe 'civilisation' and 'nature' were closer than most people thought.

Ted came into the kitchen and he opened the window. He was only about thirty, but he looked older. Tracey had never seen anyone look as sad and ashamed as Ted. There was a tension and stiffness in his body that made her feel miserable. She wanted to put her arms a-round him and hold him and tell him that everything was going to be all right in the end. But she didn't really believe that was true.

"Sorry about the smell," he said. "It's difficult without water, especially with the kids. We have to travel to my sister's place to have a proper wash. I've seen your face in the paper."

"It wasn't my real face, Ted. The face you saw, it's just a mask. A mask created by the facemakers."

Ted looked confused by this strange answer, and Tracey wasn't sure she knew what she meant herself.

Tracey went back up to her parent's flat and asked them how long Ted had been without water.

"Ted's been without water for three or four months now. He lost his job and things are hard for him. He can't pay anymore. It's hard without water."

"I know, Dad."

"It makes me mad. England's one of the richest countries in the world and some people don't even have running water anymore. There are things happening here that are all wrong. Sometimes, sometimes I think time is moving backwards, Tracey!"

He started to shake his fist in the air. He looked at her and couldn't find words to express how angry he felt.

It was strange. Charlie had also talked about England, and how he felt that time was moving backwards. Tracey remembered how hot and thirsty she'd been in the desert. How she would have sold her soul for a drink of water. But this was different. This wasn't the desert. This was England! There was plenty of water. It rained all the time, didn't it?

A terrible thought sprang into Tracey's head. Was Paul right? Was the white man's world falling apart? Was this how it happened? Not dramatically, but slowly, very slowly, day after day, things just falling apart?

Tracey opened her bag and took out her chequebook. She wrote a cheque and handed it to her Dad.

"When I'm gone, I want you to give Ted this

cheque so he can pay off his debts. Nobody should have to go without water. I know what it's like to be thirsty. When I was thirsty strangers gave me water."

"That's kind of you, Tracey. I'm really glad you haven't forgotten your roots now you're rich and famous. A tree without roots can't live. That's what my Dad always used to say."

Her dad folded the check carefully and put it in his pocket. Then he turned back to her and said something that almost made her fall through the floor.

"I was wrong about you and Pete. I threw your things out of the window and I told you to go, but I thought you'd come back. I never really wanted you to go away for good, Tracey. I'm... I'm sorry."

Tracey had never heard her father talk like this. She'd never heard him say 'sorry' to anyone.

"That's all right, Dad. That's all water under the bridge now."

Nobody said anything for a few moments. They just sat and looked at each other. Then Tracey asked her mother to tell her more about her old boyfriend, Pete.

"He's getting on well," her mother said. "He

had a lot of problems with drugs in prison, but fought against it and started to educate himself in the prison library. He's all right now and he's a got a job as a social worker. He works with young people over at the youth centre in Mill Lane."

"Is that where I can find him, Mum?"

"I think so. He's there all the time. They say he lives for his job."

"Thanks, Mum."

Tracey thanked her parents for the tea and promised to be back before ten o'clock. Then she went back down to her car and she was glad to find that it was still there and all in one piece. She drove over to Mill Lane and parked outside the youth centre.

Loud music was coming from inside and Tracey realised they were having a disco. She walked up to the door and asked two black boys if Pete was inside. They said he was and asked her why she wanted to see him. Tracey answered that she was an old friend of his. The two boys relaxed, smiled at her and told her where Pete's office was. They also told her they would look after her car. Tracey thanked them and went inside the centre.

It was very dark and the coloured lights and

the booming techno dance beat made her feel almost dizzy. She knocked on the door that said 'office', but there was no reply. Tracey turned the door handle and went inside.

She recognised Pete and saw that he was working at a computer. Tracey was surprised to see that he'd gained weight and he was going bald. His clothes were so out-of-date. Tracey smiled and remembered that Pete had always loved his long hair. Suddenly she wished she hadn't come. There was something terrible about visiting old friends.

Pete turned towards her and she could see that he recognised her.

"Tracey!"

"Hell, Pete, how are you?"

"Great, how are you? You look wonderful. You're so beautiful."

"I could be better. I've come back for a few days."

"I've seen your face so many times in the paper and on television. I told my wife that I used to know you. She doesn't really believe me. Do you want to come and have dinner with us tonight? Sara would love to meet you."

Tracey was so surprised by this shocking news

that she didn't know what to say. Suddenly, she realised that this news was not what she wanted to hear. Pete was married to somebody called Sara. Tracey hadn't expected that. Why hadn't her mum warned her? Pete? Married? Why hadn't she thought of it herself? Tracey felt stupid about everything. This wasn't part of the story she had been writing in her head.

She suddenly understood why she had come home like this, out of the blue. She had expected Pete to see her and fall in love with her all over again, just like nothing had happened. Just like they had never been apart and they were still teenagers living in the park. Tracey could see now that all that was just a romantic dream. There was going to be no 'happy ending' to the story. They were not going to hold each other, look into each other's eyes and kiss in the sunset. They were not going to go away and live happily ever after in a little cottage in the country. Pete was fat, balding and married. This was the real world.

Pete started to tell Tracey about his job and all the problems there were in the area. First there was sky-high unemployment, bad housing, poor schools, families falling apart, and massive alcohol and drug abuse. It was a catalogue of disasters and depressing to hear.

"The biggest problem is that there aren't enough jobs around here. Sometimes I think jobs are like glue in a community. Jobs hold everything together. Get rid of the 'glue' and the world starts falling to bits around your ears."

Then he started on about drugs and crime. Tracey didn't really want to hear about his job, or drugs and crime. He talked quickly and very enthusiastically, like he'd been waiting years to tell her all this. It was like sitting across from a human tidal-wave.

"You see, so many kids around here are unemployed. They're not on 'the train'. The `train' I'm talking about is society. So lots of them have built their own train. Many of them are involved in the drugs trade. That's all there is. Drugs are about the biggest 'industry' around here, and the easiest place to get a job! Sometimes it makes me want to give up."

"But you don't give up, do you, Pete?"

"No, Tracey, I don't give up. I did some bad things when I was younger. I've been in prison. I know how easy it is to get into using hard drugs. In prison I had some help. The prison governor helped me to start getting an education. Look, somebody has got to give the kids around her a chance. Help them see something positive in the world. I..."

And Pete went on and on, and Tracey stopped listening. Everything he said made sense and he was trying to do something, only Tracey hadn't really come to hear him say any of this. He didn't talk about himself or really seem interested in her feelings. All he talked about was his work and his 'mission' in life.

He started to tell her about a group of unmarried mothers who designed their own clothes and sewed them as well. Pete said how great they were and asked Tracey if she would come and see the workshop and maybe they could take some pictures of her in the clothes.

"With your face and name we could get the local press interested in the project. Will you come, Tracey?"

"I can't do it now, Pete. I'd like to help you out, but you see I'm only going to be here a short time. I have to go back to London tomorrow. It's the pressure of work. You know how it is."

"Oh no, I hoped you would be staying for a few days. I wanted you to get to know Sara and see the baby. She's called Sharon. We could have gone up into the hills for a picnic."

"Sharon? You've got a baby as well, Pete?"

"Yes, she's only three months old, cries all the time. I dream about getting a good night's sleep. I never thought having a baby was so hard."

"Yeah, it must be hard having a baby."

"I'm sorry, Tracey, I forget about... you know."

"It doesn't matter, Pete. I don't think about the baby, or the past very much."

Tracey stood up and said 'goodbye' to Pete. She promised to visit him again next time she was in Manchester. On the way back to her parent's flat she knew she would never visit Manchester again.

She slept on the sofa and couldn't sleep. Too many thoughts were racing around inside her head. Thoughts about the past, the present and the future. Tracey thought about money and the book Linda had talked about. She thought about Pete, Charlie, Paul and poor Ted. She thought about the desert, the mysterious cave and what Charlie had said about Australia. He had called it the 'future', a land of possibilities and space.

The next morning, after breakfast, Tracey said 'goodbye' to her mum and dad. She told them that next time she would ask them to come and visit her. She knew now that you couldn't turn back the clock. Seeing and hearing Pete had shown her that much.

"Where are you going now, Tracey? Got work to do?" her dad asked as she was leaving the room.

"Yes, I've got things to do, Dad. I've got some unfinished business in Australia."

"It's a shame you couldn't have stayed a bit longer," said her mum.

"I know. I'll see you both again. I promise."

At Manchester Airport Tracey telephoned London and told Linda Whitehouse her decision about the book. She would not strip naked again. She knew she would do it willingly for someone she loved, but not for the world, and certainly not for money. Linda did not say a word in reply, all Tracey heard was the 'click' of her telephone, and then absolute silence.

Afterwards Tracey bought a first class, one-way ticket for the next flight to Australia.

As she walked towards the departure-gate, she glanced at her reflection in the windows of the duty-free area. For the first time in many, many months, Tracey liked what she saw in the glass. She saw a healthy, strong-looking young woman. A woman who had proved she was brave. A woman without fear. A woman ready to face the future. Tracey smiled, raised her hand, and waved goodbye to the 'Facemakers'.

Topics and subjects in FICTION FACTORY 1-32

Topics:	FF titles:
Children	Trapped, Slaughter in Soweto
Choosing a career	The Falklands War, The Death of King Coal, The X-Rays, The Facemakers, Shadowlands
Crime	Night Attack, The Judge's Daughter, Cops and Robbers, Out of Time, The Man from Rio
Cults	Shadowlands, The Judge's Daughter, The X-Rays, The Sunnies
Dangerous jobs	The Death of King Coal, Cragscar, The Flaming Cross
Discrimination	Dreamtown, Out of Time, Witchfinder
Drugs	Black Lightning, The Judge's Daughter, Needle Street
Environmental protection	The Red Fox, The Crystal Ship, Cragscar
Film	The Judge's Daughter, Dreamtown, The Facemakers
Friendship	Christmas in Hell, The Red Fox, Women at War Dreamtown
Generation gap	The Judge's Daughter, Dreamtown, Women at War, The Sunnies
Historical events	Christmas in Hell, The Falklands War, King in a Cage, Slaughter in Soweto, Potato People, Black Lightning, The Dead Sea, The Death of King Coal
Housing	Trapped, The Flaming Cross, Dreamtown
Imperialism	King in a Cage, The Falklands War, Eldorado, Potato People
Industri and society	The Death of King Coal, Cragscar, The Dead Sea
Ireland	Potato People
Love	The X-Rays, The Death of King Coal, King in a Cage, Black Lightning, Shadowlands
Music	The X-Rays, The Judge's Daughter
New technology	Computer Kings, Dragon Rock, The Crystal Ship
New religious movements	The Sunnies
Peace/War	Dragon Rock, Christmas in Hell, Trapped, The Falklands War, King in a Cage
The press	Cops and Robbers, Eldorado

Racial segregation	Slaughter in Soweto, Out of Time, The Swordsman, King in a Cage
Racism	Night Attack, The Flaming Cross, Black Lightning, Hooligans, King in a Cage, The Swordsman
Pollution	Cragscar, The Crystal Ship, White Whales, The Dead Sea
Psychology	The Sunnies, Hooligans, Shadowlands
School	The Red Fox, The X-Rays
Science fiction	The Crystal Ship, Computer Kings, Dragon Rock, Black Lightning, White Whales
South Africa	King in a Cage, Slaughter in Soweto
Sport	Black Lightning, Hooligans, Death af King Coal
The supernatural	Witchfinder, Computer Kings, The Crystal Ship, White Whales
Violence	The Flaming Cross, Witchfinder, Women at War, Night Attack, Hooligans
Women's emancipation	Women at War, The Death of King Coal

Chart of linguistic levels in FICTION FACTORY 1-32

Elementary level:	Night Attack (FF1) The Computer Kings (FF2) Dragon Rock (FF3) The Red Fox (FF4)	Slaughter in Soweto (FF5) Christmas in Hell (FF6) Trapped (FF7) The Flaming Cross (FF8)
Pre-intermediate level:	The Sunnies (FF21) Out of Time (FF2) Hooligans (FF23) White Whales ((24)	The Dead Sea (FF25) Potato People (FF26) Eldorado (FF27) Needle Street (FF28)
Intermediate level:	The X-Rays (FF9) The Judge's Daughter (FF10) The Death og King Coal (FF11) The Falklands War (FF12) King in an Cage (FF13) Cragscar (FF14)	Cops and Robbers (FF15) Witchfinder (FF16) The Man From Rio (FF29) The Facemakers (FF30) Shadowlands (FF31) The Swordsman (FF32)
Upper intermediate level:	Women at War (FF17) The Crystal Ship (FF18) Dreamtown (FF19) Black Lightning (FF20)	

THE FACEMAKERS (Fiction Factory 30),
1. ed., 7th. imp. 2007

Author: Linda Blake
Board of editors: Jens Bendtsen, Susanne Svendsen,
Birte Hasner and Sig Krug
Linguistic consultants: Laura B. Ricks
Illustrations: Jens Lund
Lay-out: Knud Udbye
Cover design: Sig Krug
Printed in Denmark by Special-Trykkeriet Viborg a-s

Forlaget Kaleidoscope/
Kaleidoscope Publishers Ltd.
A division of Gyldendal Education
3, Klareboderne. DK 1001 Copenhagen K
Phone: (+45) 33 75 55 55. Fax: (+45) 33 75 55 44
www.gyldendal.dk/uddannelse